T H E

"I Love You" Book

THE

"I Love You" Book

More Than 500 Ways
to Show the Ones You Love
That You Care

CYNTHIA MACGREGOR AND VIC BOBB

CONARI PRESS
Berkeley, California

Conari Press books are distributed by Publishers Group West.

Cover Illustration: Rae Ecklund
Book Design: Lisa Buckley

Library of Congress Cataloging-in-Publication Data

MacGregor, Cynthia.
The "I love you" book : more than 500 ways to show the ones you love that you care / Cynthia MacGregor and Vic Bobb.
    p. cm.
  ISBN 1-57324-812-6
  1. Love—Miscellanea. I. Bobb, Vic. II. Title.
  BF575.L8 M33 2002
  152.4'1—dc21   2001005359

ISBN: 1-57324-812-6
Printed in Canada.
01 02 03 TC 10 9 8 7 6 5 4 3 2 1

T H E

"I Love You" Book

Saying "I Love You"

How—and how often—do you say, "I love you"? Whether you're thinking of your spouse or partner, your mom or dad, or your son or daughter, you probably don't get that message across often enough.

How *do* you say, "I love you"? The family of one of this book's authors says "1-4-3" for "I love you." There is one letter in "I," four in "love," and three in "you." By phrasing their "I love you"s in a cute and different way, this family gives the statement personalization and meaning.

But there are other ways of saying "I love you" besides verbally. The old song advises, "Say It with Music." The floral industry tells us to "say it with flowers." Good advice.

Another piece of good advice is the old proverb, "Actions speak louder than words." What you do for the ones you love may be the best way to say, "I love you." Not that doing meaningful things for those you love should be taken as license to *stop* saying "I love you." We all want to hear the words, too. But once you start saying "I love you" through the things you do, the possibilities become endless— and your loved ones get to feel your love through your fun or thoughtful or creative efforts. How do *you* say, "I love you"? We've got more than 500 ways for you to express your love that are more concrete, more tangible than simple words. We've given you some general ideas to start with. Knowing the person you want to convey the message to, you can probably think of still more ways.

To avoid awkward he-or-she constructions, throughout the book we've said, "Give her a . . ." or

"Take him to . . . ," but the pronouns are in most cases strictly arbitrary. Feel free to read, "Give him a . . ." or "Take her to . . . ." Few of the suggestions are truly gender-specific; most can be applied equally well to your son as to your daughter, to your mom as well as your dad, and as easily from you to your spouse or lover as from him or her to you.

So what are you waiting for? You've got a message to deliver! Whether you say it with music, with flowers, with "1-4-3" notes for your beloved, or with one of the more than 500 suggestions in this book, it's a message that will make the person you love very happy. And chances are, he or she will have something to say to you in return—verbally or otherwise.

"I love you . . . ." What a lovely message to deliver . . . however you say it.

FROM *Him to Her*
AND *Her to Him*

The words "I love you" usually come most easily to people when they're in a romantic situation, especially when love is still new. But some people have trouble saying the words even then, and others have trouble believing them.

One of us knows a woman who said, "I love you," so automatically at the end of phone conversations with her husband that one day she slipped and said it to a stranger she was ready to hang up with. While we applaud the fact that she never finished a phone conversation with her husband without an "I love you," obviously the warm closing had become rote, routine, automatic. It had ceased to have meaning. We don't applaud that.

The person you share your life with—spouse or significant other—may be starving to hear you say, "I love you," or she may hear it so often than she questions whether you mean it anymore or just say it from force of habit. Once it ceases to be meaningful, it no longer conveys the same warm feelings, the same sense of being cherished, the same weight as it did before.

4

Too, even if you say it with meaning, if your actions (or lack of them) contradict your words, the phrase will ring hollow.

- "He says he loves me, but when's the last time he actually spent an evening with me? All he does is watch TV/work on the stuff he brings home from the office/work on his silly model planes." Is that you?

- "She used to act as if I were the most important person in the world. Now she's so busy helping the kids with homework/talking to the other members of her committee on the phone all evening/writing reports that she didn't have time for at work, I have to make an appointment to have a conversation!" Is that you?

- "If he does have time to talk to me, I can tell his mind is somewhere else."

- "If she does take time to talk, she's so tired, it's not much of a conversation."

Sometimes we can't help the distractions of real life that interfere with our time with the ones we really care about. Of course, we need to make time to be with those we love . . . and not just time but (pardon an overworked expression) quality time. That's the subject of another book, though. But we can do the little things that show the ones we love that we care about them.

Most women don't need a tennis bracelet or a diamond ring as proof of love—a single rose when it isn't her birthday (and when the rose isn't a guilt offering) will go far toward showing her you were thinking about her, you care, you really do love her. (Although we're about to offer you some suggestions that are far less timeworn than roses.)

And men appreciate little proofs of affection too. It can be something as simple as a new bag of golf balls, a luxurious massage from your loving hands on a night when he's extra-tired, or a love note left on his pillow, detailing some—or even just one—of the reasons you love him.

Whether you're a new couple, looking to make each other understand that love is in your hearts, or whether you've been together for several decades and you want to convey that the love that first brought you together is still verdant in your heart of hearts, you need to get the message across, you need to do it believably, and you need to do it even when it isn't an anniversary or other occasion.

Here are some ideas:

*I*f you have a big budget, rent a nearby billboard and use it to proclaim your love for your beloved in large letters. You can write a clever message or a simple "Craig loves Emily . . . THIS MUCH!"

*Write him a love letter—
when it's not a birthday or
anniversary.*

Get up 10 minutes early and start the coffee.

Take a cue from David Letterman and present your loved one with a list: Top Ten Reasons Why I Love You. (If you think of more than ten good reasons, throw them in and call them Bonus Reasons.)

With a kettle half-full of warm water, give her a nice footbath while she's watching TV. Leave her feet wrapped in a fluffy, woolly towel while you go get her a bowl of ice cream.

Next Valentine's Day, buy an extra card. Send it to her in August or October.

Cook him a special dinner. Serve it on a tablecloth instead of place mats, and decorate the table, too, with flowers, seashells, pine branches, or candles.

Repot those plants she has been meaning to get to for weeks.

When she's sick, buy her three or four magazines on a topic that intrigues her, such as home decorating, doll making, quilting, horses, or wherever her interests lie.

If you have adequate computer experience, you can change his screen saver. Next time he's sitting there in front of the computer, daydreaming or trying to figure out how to finish that paragraph, instead of those goofy fish swimming tirelessly back and forth on the screen, he'll find himself confronted with big letters that announce, "Evan, You Are the Light of My Life!"

Say "I love you" by making a CD or tape that is a collection of those very special songs that help define you as a couple in love. If you don't have CD-burning capacity, you can make a tape, or ask around—one of your friends almost certainly has a CD burner.

Give him the window seat.

Go for a walk in the rain together.

Arrange for him to drive some of that big earth-moving equipment he's always saying *Wow!* about.

Have her car detailed.

While you're out of town, conspire with a friend to have the friend tape to your beloved's front door every night (or put through the mail slot, if you have one, or slide under the door if possible) an envelope containing one in a series of love notes you'll have left behind for that purpose.

If she wakes up to the same radio station every morning, find out what it would cost to buy 15 seconds of advertising time and surprise her with an on-the-air love note.

13

Keep all ticket stubs, motel receipts, and other paper mementos of the trips and special activities that have helped make life with your loved one delightful. Mount or display them in an original way—such as on a piece of colored poster board, or decoupaged to a wooden cutting board, or under lacquer or glass on a coffee table. Emphasize that the other person is a huge part of the reason that the trip or event was special.

Buy six rolls of Scotch tape before Christmas.

Have a quartet serenade your loved one at work, at the hairdresser's, down at the pier where he's fishing, or some other place outside the house where you know your beloved will be.

Write "I love you" instead of "Wash me" in the dirt on the big back hatch door of the van.

Have a T-shirt printed with your
pet name for her on it.

If he listens to cassettes on his drive to
work, make a tape of a nice speech
that tells him how much you love him
and why. Slip it into the tape player in
his car one night, and your voice will
give him a surprise boost when he
heads off to work in the morning.

Bring her breakfast in bed.

Give him a certificate for a hot air balloon ride.
Not on a special occasion . . . just because.

Using your computer, post a message
declaring your love on an online
forum.

Serenade her . . . under a window, if possible.
That's a lovely way to say, "I love you."

Treat her to a special dinner on the anniversary of your first date.

If she listens to homemade music tapes, find a tape that has a few moments of silence at the end, and record your own surprise message.

Write a song about your beloved. If you can't write music, set the words to an existing tune. It doesn't have to be Grammy-winning quality; it just has to come from your heart.

Take out a classified ad declaring your love in your local paper's Announcements section.

Hire a skywriter to declare your love on the largest "blackboard" in existence.

Buy her a single bud rose, and give it to her with a note that says, "Like this rose, our love is only beginning to blossom. May it unfold into a thing of beauty for many years."

Give her some spice potpourri with a note saying, "You are the spice of my life."

Instead of an anniversary card, send him a list headed, "Reasons Why I'd Marry You All Over Again."

Bring him a gift, or cook her a special dinner, to celebrate other "anniversaries," such as the anniversary of the day you met, the day you/she/he proposed, or your first date.

Use colored icing to write "I love you" on top of a cake.

On her birthday—or on any ordinary day that you want to make a little special—fill the tub with bubble bath and then bring her a glass of still more bubbles—champagne—that she can enjoy while she luxuriates in the tub. Offer to wash her back . . . or to leave her alone to enjoy the interior and exterior bubbles in blissful solitude.

21

Send him love notes that have been sprayed with his favorite perfume, addressed to him at work.

Don't throw away his disreputable old shirt.

Stop by the video store and pick up that movie he's been wanting to see.

With a fork, poke "I love you" in the top of an apple pie before baking it.

Buy her a manicure.

Go out to look at the stars together.

Give her the piece of cake with the extra icing on it.

Buy a gift certificate for an hour-long massage.

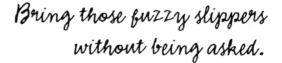

Bring those fuzzy slippers without being asked.

Let him watch his favorite show even though it comes on at the same time as yours.

Read the same book, and talk about it.

Hire a baby-sitter on the sly, and surprise her with a night out.

Watch a ballgame with her, and cheer for her team.

25

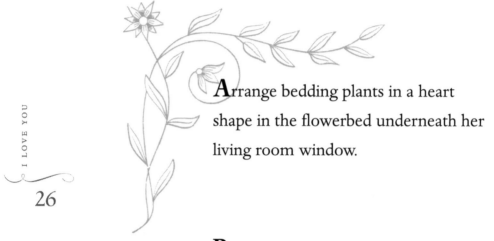

Arrange bedding plants in a heart shape in the flowerbed underneath her living room window.

Buy him the latest issue of his favorite magazine.

Stick an "I love you" note on his steering wheel while he's at work.

Write "I love you" with a felt-tip on a deflated balloon; have him blow it up at bedtime.

Replace the batteries in the smoke detector.

Push the self-cleaning oven button on your way to work.

27

Plant petunias, pansies, zinnias, and marigolds to spell out your initials, then a plus sign, then his initials.

Buy her a back-scratcher for when you're not around.

Play a card game that you used to play.

Re-create your honeymoon.

Wash her car.

Write the story of your first date (or of some other significant experience early in your relationship) as a chapter in a romance novel or a story in a magazine. Cast it in the third person: "As Chris first tasted Kim's lips, it was as though the skies had opened and a choir of angels were singing the 'Ode to Joy' from Beethoven's *Ninth Symphony*."

Clean the algae from his aquarium.

Write what you would put on the dedication page of your novel.

Apologize for having acted like a jerk Thursday night.

Give your beloved a copy of *Sonnets from the Portuguese* by Elizabeth Barrett Browning.

Help him research his family tree.

Insert into a folded-up shirt or pair of underwear in his drawer a note that reads, "This certificate good for a special treat tonight, just to show you how much I love you," and be prepared to make good on the promise. It's up to you to decide what the "special treat" should be.

Have your portrait taken and framed.

Put a new bottle of shampoo within reach of the shower, with an "I love you" sign on a string around the bottle.

Give her the top half of a pair of your pajamas on a cold night.

Don't roll your eyes when he tells that joke . . . again.

Praise her cooking when dinner's good . . . and don't make a fuss when it falls short of your expectations.

With glow-in-the-dark paint that will be invisible in the daylight, paint "I love you" on the white ceiling above his bed.

Arrange to have a romantic message flashed on the scoreboard at halftime of the homecoming game.

*Take her for a ride
on a carousel.*

Write a poem for her—even if it's pure doggerel, even if it's only four lines long, even if you've never written a poem before.

Bake fortune cookies that contain special "I love you" messages.

Kidnap her from work. Make arrangements secretly, getting things fixed so she can be spirited away from the office, taken to the already-reserved room at the ski inn, and kept there for a surprise weekend dedicated to finding nice ways (new and old both) to say "I love you."

Insert an "I love you" message at the beginning of her favorite videotaped movie. (You'll dub it in over the opening credits, or ads, or previews . . . but not over the opening of the movie!)

Buy him new sheets.

Let her sleep in, and you take the kids to early morning choir practice.

Hire somebody to wash her windows.

Change her oil and rotate her tires . . . then top it off by taking her out to dinner.

Give him something engraved with his initials . . . or, better yet, with a few meaningful words of love.

Wear your hair the way she likes it.

Play strip cribbage, bridge, dominoes, poker, or whatever.

Don't say a thing when she loses her car keys (again).

Write "I love you" on the mirror with shaving cream.

Buy him new shoelaces.

Take the kids to breakfast, and bring her breakfast back so that she doesn't have to leave her bed.

Rent a bicycle built for two.

Put the last ice cubes in *her* lemonade instead of yours.

Put the lid back onto the salsa *(again)*, and don't say anything about it.

Flip the car radio back to her station when you park for the night.

Do a cross-stitch of his fraternity seal.

Brush or comb your hair before breakfast.

Alphabetize her CD collection.

Read aloud from her favorite book while she's in the bathtub.

Don't say anything about the fact that he hasn't touched that expensive wind-surfing equipment for three years.

When she gets home from work, have the kids already at a sitter's, the candles lit, the champagne chilled, and dinner cooking.

When she says, "Isn't she beautiful?," reply,
"Nah—not my type."

Give her a rose for every year you've been married.

*Scoot the driver's seat back—
or forward—if she's going to
be the next one to use the car.*

Learn how to say "I love you" in as many other languages as possible. (*Sources:* Local embassies, foreign language dictionaries, friends and neighbors from foreign countries.) Leave *"Je t'aime"* notes in foreign languages, or murmur *"Te adoro"* and its various equivalents in your beloved's ear.

Show interest in his hobby, even if a collection of surfboard fins ranks right up there, to you, with lug-nuts.

Make her a bead necklace, even though you're probably no better at that kind of craft now than you were when you were at summer camp.

Tell her how much better she looks than all those women in the magazine ads.

Go window shopping with her, and don't complain or look impatient (or look pointedly patient).

Kiss her in the elevator on the way to the accountant's office.

Put the cap back on the toothpaste.

Buy your partner some high-quality golf balls.

Give him a poster of his favorite linebacker.

Watch some meaningless Sunday afternoon TV together.

Clean out her car for her.

Put an "I love you" note in the pocket of the shirt he'll be wearing to work tomorrow.

Give him a list of the best of the fun
and funny things you've done together.

Write "I love you" with food coloring in the snow.

Run her baby picture in a newspaper ad, along
with an "I Love You" message.

FROM *Adult Children* TO *Parents*

"Actions speak louder than words" may be a cliché, but there's a reason for that. Clichés *become* clichés through frequent repetition . . . and most expressions that get repeated till they're shopworn are oft said simply because they're true.

What do *your* actions say? Do they say, "I love you" . . . or do they say, "I take you for granted"? (Do they say anything at all?) There are plenty of ways to show your love to your parents. There are plenty of ways to show them you still treasure them, that they are still important to you, even though you're no longer a child.

When you were a kid, you probably made your mother and father some wonderful "treasures" in school, camp, or Scouts. Did your mother lovingly display a misshapen vase you'd created in arts and crafts (and did she use it to hold dandelions you'd picked for her)?

The vase, and the dandelions too, were all gifts that said, "I love you." It's a message your parents still want to hear. Unless you happen to be a pottery enthusiast, you probably no longer craft vases. Fortunately, though, that isn't the only way for you to get the message across. In fact, as an adult, you have a plethora of ways to show your parents that you care.

There are things you can make for them, things you can do for them, things (other than "I love you," in so many words) that you can say to them.

But do you? Or do you assume, "They know I love them"? Don't assume. Don't take your parents for granted . . . or even let it appear that you do. Every day is precious. Every day is a new opportunity to show them that you care, that you appreciate them, that you're aware of the things they did for you and still do. Every day is a new opportunity to show your parents that you truly love them.

No matter the other relationships that enter into your life—friends, spouses or other partners, even your own children—your parents will always be of prime importance to you. They raised you. They were there for you all through your childhood. They still are.

Show them you haven't forgotten. Here are some ways of getting the message across. Some of them apply specifically to parents who live nearby; some apply to parents who live at a distance; some will work in either case. Some are more applicable to young parents (you're in your twenties and they're in their forties); others are more suited to parents who are slowing down in their lifestyles and perhaps their abilities. But whatever your parents' age or situation, and wherever they live, you'll find in the section that follows a wealth of ways to say "I love you" to the people most responsible for making you what you are today.

Assemble a scrapbook of memorabilia that is meaningful to your mom and dad. Include written tributes such as "Why Dad Is the Greatest" from as many family members as you can get to participate.

Make a charitable contribution to an organization in honor of your parents. Don't wait till their fiftieth anniversary—or their death—to memorialize them.

Next Mother's Day or Father's Day, write a letter to the editor of your parents' local paper, paying tribute to how well your mom or dad raised you.

The next time you know Mom and Dad are going to dinner at their favorite restaurant, call ahead and make arrangements to have a bottle of champagne served to them.

Rent a billboard that says, "[Your parents' names] Are the World's Greatest Parents." Be sure it's somewhere near their home, so not only will they see it but their neighbors and nearby friends will too.

Make a birthday or anniversary party for one or both parents, and make a big deal out of it even when it isn't a "milestone" birthday or anniversary.

Give Mom a pedicure yourself.

Write a thank-you letter to your folks. You've acknowledged Aunt Edna's crocheted sweaters and Great Aunt Edith's inedibly rock-hard cookies faithfully every year, but did you ever tell your parents how much you appreciated their always being there for you? Being patient through your rebellious years? Letting you borrow the car again even after the Infamous Disaster? Putting you through college? Raising you to be, all things considered, a reasonably decent citizen? Not micro-managing the way you raise your kids? (If they're not batting 1,000 on all these items, at least thank them for what they've succeeded at.)

Take a Sunday afternoon to clean your parents' house.

Say "I love you" by thinking of a labor-saving, time-saving, or problem-solving device you could buy, build, create, or invent to help make your mom's or dad's life easier. Then buy or build it now, without waiting for the next official gift-giving occasion.

What are your parents' interests? What does their home need? What, if any, are their physical limitations or restrictions? Whether you build them some shelves, buy your dad a useful gadget for fishermen, or find the ideal device to help your mom through her daily routine despite her arthritis, the gift will be specific to their needs—and the fact that it comes not at a holiday or birthday but on an "any day" makes it all the more meaningful.

Take out a classified ad or, if you can afford it, a small display ad in your local newspaper, congratulating your mom or dad on their birthdays, or thanking them on Mothers' Day or Fathers' Day for all they've done for you.

Every now and then, instead of phoning your folks, write a letter. Your parents can't re-listen to a phone call the way they can re-read and savor, pass around, and save a letter.

Quit smoking.

Cook their favorite meal . . . the one that's too much trouble for Mom to bother with for just the two of them.

Pay for their cable TV a year in advance.

Say "I love you" by sending your folks a plane ticket to come visit you—with open dates so they can pick a time that's convenient for them as well as for you.

61

Bring your recipe box on your next trip so you can treat them to a few nights of your favorite meals . . . and treat Mom and Dad to a few nights out of the kitchen.

Clean, vacuum, wash, and wax your parents' car.

Locate Mom's long-lost best friend from way-back-when, or Dad's old Army buddy, and reunite them, if only by mail.

Make them a crossword puzzle filled with clues and words that only a family member could get.

Take your dad out on your new boat, just the two of you. (And then invite him to bring along one of his friends next time.)

Draw a picture of the most precious family-related memory from your childhood.

Split enough firewood to get them all the way through next winter.

Have the radio station they listen to congratulate them on their anniversary.

Give them binoculars and a book about birds to get them started on a new hobby.

Make a "Mom—Your Life" or "Dad—Your Life" video. Interview family members who can talk about their memories of Mom or Dad. Get siblings, parents, kids, grandkids—everyone—into the act. If significant friends and even treasured neighbors, present or past, are available to be interviewed, include them too. If feasible, include footage of houses Mom or Dad lived in previously, schools they attended, and as much more as you can.

Prune your parents' flowers, clip their hedges, mow their lawn, or weed their lawn or flowerbed.

Assemble a multi-generational family photo album. Include your parents' ancestors from as far back as you have pictures, as well as cousins and aunts and uncles, your parents' siblings, and yourselves, your siblings, and your children, nieces, and nephews.

Wash your parents' windows . . . inside and out.

Give your mother a gift on *your* birthday. After all, she's the one who brought you into this world to begin with, and she deserves to be celebrated on your birthday. Without her there would be no you. And without her raising you, you might have turned out very differently.

Clean out your folks' attic—but do more than just clean it out and get rid of the no-longer-neededs. Salvage and work on any real treasures you find up there, and present them to your folks. This might include cleaning and oiling Dad's old baseball glove from his childhood (or his brief career in the minor leagues) and presenting it to him to display in his den; decoratively framing a doily that Mom got as a wedding present forty years ago; or putting your christening outfit on a baby doll and giving it to Mom to display in her bedroom or family room.

If your religious or personal beliefs preclude your naming your child after a living relative, but you want to honor your mother in naming your daughter, consider naming her after your mom's favorite flower, gem, or bird. Or honor your dad by naming your daughter "Violet" after the color of his eyes, or nickname your son "Ram" or "Steele" in honor of Dad's favorite team.

Make a kid-style homemade valentine out of construction paper cut into a heart with a paper lace doily glued on. On it, express your loving sentiments in your own words . . . not the fabricated one-size-fits-all sentiments of a commercial greeting card company.

Buy your folks a CD, cassette, or even LP of music from their era. Check for used records/tapes/discs, too, at thrift shops or yard sales.

Give them a present when it isn't an occasion—just because you love them and were thinking of them.

Print out, on your computer, an official-looking certificate proclaiming your folks "Best Parents Ever."

Honor your parents by writing a family history of both sides of the family and passing it along to your kids, thus guaranteeing that your parents and their ancestors will be kept alive in writing and in clear family memories, even after they're no longer around.

Collect your mom's favorite maxims and beliefs, turning them into a homemade "booklet," however small. Print the pages out, and make the cover out of cardboard or tagboard covered in gift wrap or spare wallpaper. Pass the booklet on to your child, or keep it in the family library, showing your mom that all her lessons weren't lost on you.

Take a good picture—possibly even a formal portrait—of your parents, have it enlarged to at least 8" x 10" and framed, and place it in a prominent position of honor in your living room or other suitable site.

Collect family stories about your parents' childhood from their parents or other relatives, in writing or recorded on an audiocassette or CD.

Organize your parents' collection of loose photos into a proper album, labeling the pictures informatively whenever possible.

Send Mom a singing telegram. Have the messenger sing a medley beginning with "M-O-T-H-E-R" ("M is for the many things she gave me"), and continuing with Mom's favorite song, followed by any other songs you can think of that seem appropriate.

Compile a tape of your dad's favorite songs—possibly leading into each with a DJ-style dedication, all to him, each from you, each specifying a different reason for the dedication ("To Dad from Kelly, for letting me follow my dream, even though you would have liked me to be a lawyer like you"; "To Dad from Kelly, for not lecturing me that time I scraped your new car's fender").

Buy your mom a copy of that book you just read that you loved so much. Be sure to inscribe it with a note from you on the title page.

Buy your mom a bouquet of her favorite flowers—for no reason except that you love her and knew she'd enjoy them.

Send a postcard every Tuesday on which you have written one wonderful memory from your growing-up years.

*Buy Mom a new set of pots
and pans to replace that
well-worn collection that's
seen better days.*

If your parents' place is small, stay in a motel when you go to visit them, so that you don't disrupt their daily routine.

Prune all their potted plants, and repot the ones that are getting root-bound.

Change the oil in their car . . . and in the lawn mower and snow blower, too.

Even though you're all grown up, take a vacation with your parents.

Remember when you were a child, and your mom or dad would banish the bogeyman by fixing or changing the things that scared you? Oiling the door hinge that squeaked scarily, cutting the limb off the tree that cast weird shadows on your shade? Your turn to take care of the things that concern them!

Clean the gutters, so they don't have to worry about water accumulations, and fix that shutter that bangs every time the wind blows.

Buy her a "World's Greatest Mom" coffee cup . . . even if she always said, "Those things are so tacky."

Keep and share a thorough record of all the cute things the grandkids say. (And that includes the second, third, and fourth grandkid—not just the first one!)

Create a banner of her favorite motto, to show it sank in after all those years.

Teach him how to use a computer for writing his memoirs.

Send postcards from wherever you go—even if it's just across town. In L.A. or Omaha on business? Even if you called Mom to let her know you landed safely, send her a postcard to let her know you were thinking of her after that, too. Downtown for a business lunch? Send a postcard uptown to the Upper East Side and show Dad his all-grown-up child is still his kid and still thinks of him. (You might even help Mom and Dad start a new hobby— collecting postcards.)

Give them a box full of stamps, envelopes, and stationery so that it's easy for them to stay in touch with you. (Even if buying the stamps is no financial hardship for them, standing in line to buy them isn't fun at any age.)

When Mom offers to fuss in the kitchen, fixing your favorite meal, don't protest. Let her feel she still has the ability to spoil you. But offer to lend a hand peeling the potatoes or chopping the veggies—the "chore" parts of the cooking—leaving just the creative parts for Mom.

When Dad tells the story of that camping trip and embellishes the cute thing you said when the storm hit, don't correct him.

Create and frame an artistic collage of family photos that your parents can hang with pride.

Without waiting for Christmas or a birthday, give a magazine subscription.

Really do pay attention when your mom is explaining how to quilt.

Arrange for their next batch of checks to be something other than those boring blue ones they've insisted are just fine ever since 1964.

Give them a packet of "Thank You" notes the day of their retirement party or fiftieth anniversary celebration.

Read those health-oriented clippings Mom keeps sending you, and discuss them with her so she knows you've read them.

Write them a letter telling the reasons you're glad that they're your parents.

Bring over to their home a meal you've made that contains things you're pretty sure are not part of their usual menu.

Dedicate your book to your parents.

Buy a lottery ticket for them every week.

Leave an "I love you" note in the freezer on top of the packages of homegrown rhubarb.

Get them season tickets to their favorite team.

If fortune has been good to you, spring for a swimming pool in their back yard.

Clean out their garage. Then hold a garage sale, and present Mom and Dad with the proceeds, "for your vacation fun" (or "for a night out at a nice restaurant," or whatever you know they'd enjoy). And now that the garage is clean again, does the inside need painting?

Make a "family" wall in your house that's covered with photographs of your distant relatives, your childhood, and your immediate family. If your folks are knocked out by it, have copies made for their own wall.

Drop in on them periodically with your sewing kit, and ask what needs mending.

Treat them each to a professional massage.

When they visit from out of town, have balloons, streamers, and a "Welcome" banner to greet them.

Spend the evening swapping stories about pets from long ago.

Buy them some gourmet foods or fancy coffee, an extravagance they might not allow themselves.

Treat your mom to a day at the spa.

Have all their family movies transferred to videotape.

Ask what they need to have done around the house, and if you can't do it yourself or don't live nearby, pay to have it done professionally.

Get them some nice lawn chairs and patio furniture.

Pay for health club memberships for them.

Go along and keep them company when they go to the barber or hairdresser.

Provide them with a big box of wrapping paper, ribbons, tape, and so on. And a selection of greeting cards for all kinds of occasions.

89

Save coupons for them.

Buy them those end tables they were admiring longingly in the antique shop.

Send them to DisneyWorld or Epcot.

Pay for a Defensive Driving for Seniors course for both your parents . . . and insist they attend.

Buy them a computer and get them software for one of the online services. Make sure there's e-mail from you waiting for them the very first day they're online, and keep the mail coming regularly after that . . . even if they only live across town.

Take their newspapers, glass, and aluminum cans to the recycling center.

Thank them for letting you have a dog as a child.

Send good videotapes of the grandchildren.

Start a stamp collection for your dad. Perhaps make it a specialty collection—stamps from his ancestors' homelands, U.S. commemoratives, misprints, or rarities. Give him the necessary equipment plus a few stamps to get started. If he's a history buff, point out, if he hasn't realized this before, the way that stamps commemorate people, places, and events in a nation's history. Or start a coin collection for him, with coins of many nations and many denominations, all dated from his birth year.

Take your mom to spend an afternoon at an art museum.

Buy them a book of crossword puzzles.

Has your mom been asking you, every time her old friends come for a dinner party—the ones who "remember you when"—to please drop in for half an hour? Yes, she wants to show you off, and no, it won't be fun, but this time, show up anyhow.

Get your kids to tape a birthday message to Grandma or Grandpa. It's a greeting they can keep and treasure for years.

Buy them a satellite dish—and install it, too, or pay for professional installation.

Have copies made of those fading old cardboard-mounted photographs of their parents and from their childhoods. The photo processor will have to create new negatives, which can be stored away for safekeeping, then can make new pictures that can be framed (in better condition than the original pictures) or used in a family album or one of the other projects listed in this book.

Tell them all about your very favorite childhood birthday and what made it so special.

Send them a bouquet of flowers for no reason.

Buy them a cordless phone. The living room phone may not reach Dad's recliner. Mom may not be able to get out of the tub in time to catch an incoming call as easily as she used to. They both can bring it with them when they're puttering in their garden— or when Dad's in the garage, tinkering, or when Mom's in the attic, looking for the winter clothes she stored up there.

Make sure your kids write thank-you notes to your parents in a timely manner.

Buy them new tools when the old ones are worn out.

Make tapes of the interesting wildlife documentaries that come in on the channel that they don't get.

Send them a box of paperback books.

Drive them to the polls on Election Day.

Get them a bottle of the wine that they love but never think it's sensible to buy.

Give them a parakeet that says, "I love you."

Arrange for them to get ATM bank cards, and teach them how to get money from the machines, even on the weekend.

Tell them three of the happiest memories you have of growing up.

Help them program their phone for speed dialing.

Cross-stitch a "Home Sweet Home" hanging that lists all the addresses your family has ever had.

Bring Great Aunt Vivian in from the rest home, to save your folks the drive across town (and to give them all a visit in more homey surroundings).

Get them a couple of their favorite books on audiotape or CD for their next car trip.

Introduce them to Post-It notes.

Straighten up the garden shed—including transferring potting soil and fertilizer from those torn old paper bags into plastic buckets.

Have a hand-tinted copy made of that old picture of Great-Grandma and Great-Grandpa back when they were homesteading in the Dakotas.

Help them learn how to program their VCR.

Give them several packets of flower seeds.

Give them a package of ballpoint pens and a package of automatic pencils.

101

Take their laundry to the cleaner's.

Send a box of chocolates even though it's not Valentine's Day, Mother's or Father's Day, or any other occasion.

Don't make fun of the music they listen to.

Make a nice framed display of all the grandkids' school pictures.

Help make that canal cruise they've been planning for months stress-free by taking care of arrangements for lawn care and paper and mail delivery.

Give them one of those beaded cushions to sit on in the car.

Organize the tools in the workshop in the basement.

Make a bunch of homemade dinners for them to keep handy in the freezer.

Give Dad a list of the things you're most glad you did together while you were growing up.

Get two copies made of every roll of pictures of your kids, and give a set to Mom and Dad.

Take the stuff in the corner of the garage to Goodwill.

Get more exercise, and let them know that you're bringing your cholesterol down.

Help them organize and label that box full of snapshots.

Knit them really soft, warm mufflers.

FROM *Parents* TO *Adult Children*

Of course you love your kids as much as always, and of course they know that . . . right? Well, they may know it intellectually . . . but do they feel it emotionally?

After all their complaining, you've finally learned to hold yourself in check; you've finally stopped babying them. It took an effort, but you stopped calling your twenty-one-year-old, living-on-her-own daughter after dates to make sure she'd gotten home safely and nothing had gone awry. You stopped suggesting that your son, then twenty-eight, come home to his old room every time he had a little sniffle, so you could take care of him. You stopped offering to do your youngest child's laundry even before she moved out of town.

To you, these were things you did not only to satisfy your own needs but to show you love your kids. Lee may be twenty-eight now, or forty-two, but Lee will always be your baby. At twenty-eight or forty-two, though, Lee doesn't want to be babied anymore.

And yet . . . there are times when, even though your son or daughter is grateful for finally being treated like an adult, she misses the message of love that was inherent in all the fussing and checking and questioning you did. If you've finally learned to stop asking frequently, "Are you eating healthily? Are you getting enough sleep?" your grown child may have mixed emotions. He may be glad . . . and yet miss the underlying love expressed in that message.

Fortunately there are plenty of other ways to say "I love you" to your grown kids . . . ways that don't smother, don't rob your children of their independence, don't embarrass them in front of their friends. There are things you can do for them or say to them that have the clear subtext of "I love you. I care how you are. I'm proud of you." (And if once in a while, you ask if your daughter is getting enough rest and enough vitamins, or you ask your son if he's okay for money, that's all right too.)

*T*ell your daughter what a good mother she is; tell her you couldn't do a better job yourself.

Buy a Savings Bond a month for a year, then present them to your child on July 4.

Write a little essay or letter called, "Why I'm Glad You're My Kid," and mail it to your daughter at her place of work.

Frame a collage or other arrangement of all of his school pictures, perhaps with a graduation or commencement picture as the centerpiece.

Send care packages when their lives are frantic. There's nothing like a couple of jars of Mom's raspberry jam, some new cloth napkins, and a bag of homemade cookies to put that dispute with the Business Office into perspective. And to say "I love you" to your daughter or son at a time when he or she may need to hear it the most.

113

*Have some really nice
return-address labels
made for them.*

Call at convenient times . . . not at 7:40 A.M. when the kids are late for the school bus.

Don't complain about her husband's messy habits.

Offer to baby-sit when you haven't been asked.

Give your grown child a "report card," showing as subjects all the good qualities, attributes, or accomplishments she has to her credit, and grading her "A+" on each.

Preserve a whole extra batch of peaches next summer, and sneak all the home-canned goodies into your child's house.

Write a poem praising your child. It doesn't have to be long or fancy. It doesn't even have to be perfect. It just has to come from your heart.

Tell him why you're proud of him, not when he's just accomplished something special, but on an ordinary day.

Drop off a homemade dinner at your son's or daughter's house, along with some romantic candles. Turn right around and leave, taking their kids with you for the evening. Leave your son or daughter and spouse to a romantic evening alone, with a delicious, homemade, no-cooking dinner to enjoy. Return the kids just in time for their bedtime—or, even better, do it on a night when there's no school the next day, and keep the kids overnight.

Go over and help repot those houseplants.

Arrange to have the fusebox in that old house replaced with circuit breakers.

Provide a "Call home" phone card.

Tell him how proud you were when he made First Class in Scouts.

Give her a big bottle of vitamins.

Help out so she can afford a top-of-the-line battery for her car.

Make maple sugar candy for his birthday.

Don't emphasize how jerky you think the guy is whom she voted for.

Copy those All-Time Favorite recipes to give your newly liberated offspring a tasty tie to her growing-up days.

Write your memoirs, autobiography, reminiscences, or whatever you want to call them. Put them into a book form, including photographs, and present this very special little volume to your kids.

Say "I love you" by telling her that you hope her kids turn out half as well as she did.

Give her fifteen stamped, addressed envelopes so she can drop you a note every couple of days.

Pay their car insurance for the next three months.

Put to work your years of expertise at
making the best of crummy places,
and go help with paint and wallpaper.

Send a just-for-no-reason "I Love You" card.

Frame and present him with a piece of artwork he
did when he was six.

Lend them the motorhome for a week.

Don't tell them how silly you think that fashion looks.

Write down all the stories your parents told you about their childhoods and give them to your kids, to create a link between them and their past.

Try not to start any sentences on child-raising with, "When you were [their child's] age . . . ."

Make and present an elegant certificate celebrating what a Great Kid you have.

Put some money against the principal on their mortgage.

Give her dog a really upscale chew toy.

Take five rolls of pictures of their kids, and have the best ones blown up to 9" x 12" size.

Find a beautiful silver filigree candle for the mantel.

Have those battered copies of *Just-So Stories* and *The Wind in the Willows* repaired, or even re-bound.

Give her the extra money so their new car can have cloth seats.

Recommend a trustworthy broker.

Pay your child's rent or mortgage payment one month.

Pay for a Weekend Getaway. If your grown child is married, see if you can swing payment for both of them to go away together, even if it's just to a modestly priced, nearby place to bring the cost within affordable limits. If your kid has kids of his own, the getaway will be even more appreciated. (Of course, single people need a break in the routine, too, so we're by no means suggesting this only for your married kids.)

The key word is *getaway*—the destination doesn't have to be a fabulous (and fabulously expensive) resort; a cozy bed-and-breakfast or a modestly priced inn will do quite nicely, as long as it's a change of scene.

Write down all those stories that Grandma told, and that have continued to exist only as oral tales. This is a gift not only for your child but for posterity—for your children's children (present or future), and on beyond. If you have a computer, type the stories on it and print out multiple copies. You can save them in "book" form, either in a loose-leaf notebook or held together with a report fastener or in a binder (both available at your local office supply store).

127

Give your kid the booties in which he came home from the hospital.

Write a letter to your grandchildren telling how much you value and love their folks. Include some nice specific stories about what a treat your kids were to have around when they were growing up.

Give him some good advice about investments . . . but don't bug him about following up on it.

Do the dishes after you have dinner at your child's place.

Get coupons for professional portraits of your daughter and her family.

If you drop in on your daughter, and the atmosphere is either heavy with contention or smoky with eroticism, know that you've picked a bad time, and leave even if your daughter protests, "No—stay. It's fine."

Give them a smoke alarm for every floor of their house—including the basement.

Keep his dog the week he takes the family to Disneyland.

Help organize all that jumbled-together fabric in her sewing room.

Buy CDs to replace some of his old Rolling Stones LPs.

Buy him another computer so he doesn't have to fight the kids for a chance to work at it (or play on it).

Order one of those "What happened the day you were born" front-page reprints for your son.

Give him your good old thimble—even if he doesn't sew. It will be a loving memento.

If your daughter's insurance doesn't cover mammograms, pay for her to get one, and keep her company when she goes for her next test.

Get her a new head cleaner for the cassette deck in her car.

Tell stories about when you were growing up. As an adult, he can appreciate those stories more than he could as a kid, so tell them again even if he's heard them before. The more the world changes, the more meaningful such stories of "the old times" become—and the older your grown kids get, the more meaningful the stories become on a personal level.

When you're going to the supermarket, call and ask, "Can I pick up anything for you while I'm at the store?"

Rent a steam carpet cleaner and clean the rugs and seats in the van.

Have Grandpa's pocket watch refurbished and give it to your son on what would have been Grandpa's birthday.

Take your kid to the ball game . . . and sit in the good seats, this time, instead of the bleachers that are all he usually can afford.

Buy a bird feeder she can place outside the window she sits next to most frequently.

Give a pair of bookends with your and your spouse's pictures laminated onto the outside surface of the wood.

Sing him the story song that you used to use to fill the miles between home and Grandma's house.

Don't just pass down Grandma's recipes to your daughter. Show her the little kitchen tricks Grandma taught you: the secret to getting cakes to rise so high, the time-saving and labor-saving short-cuts, and yes, the extra-work-requiring secrets of special cookery, too.

Be patient when he talks about RAM and MEGs and hard drives and nonsense like that when all you want to learn is how to turn on the machine and type a letter to your sister in Cleveland.

Replace the washer so the faucet doesn't drip anymore.

Make a big fuss over his thirtieth, fortieth, or fiftieth birthday. Throw him a party and ask people to come with stories about why they love him.

Help her remember a scary milestone happily. It could be something as mild as a significant birthday or something as serious as a life-threatening illness—her own, her spouse's, her child's—or a death in the family. By concentrating on the bright side of it (eventual recovery from an illness, lessons learned from a bad experience, advances in life achieved by the time of the birthday), help her to see the positive side of the event.

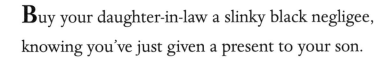
*When your kid calls long
distance, have him hang up,
and you call back so it's
"your nickel."*

Buy your daughter-in-law a slinky black negligee,
knowing you've just given a present to your son.

Get into that trunk under the stairs and show him
your merit badges from Scouts.

Don't complain about the radio station your kid is listening to while visiting you and lying around on the deck.

Let her read the letters you and your spouse exchanged while you were courting.

Have a print shop make your son a calendar that uses photographs from his childhood.

Encourage your child to start playing piano again, even if the last lesson was back in sixth grade, thirty years ago.

Arrange for a mini-family reunion: Have a big picnic at the park along the river and get as many of you together as possible. Eat good food and throw Frisbees and laugh a lot and enjoy being a family.

Hire an artist to give your child oil-painting lessons.

Give your child a letter that you might have written to him or her in the week before the child was born. The letter can express the hopes and love and expectations and trepidations that you felt before this new life came into the world.

Then append to that letter a piece that tells your child how wonderfully he or she has fulfilled and exceeded your hopes and expectations.

Get the whole family together—including in-laws and grandkids—and have professional portraits taken.

Pay for your child to take a self-defense class.

Don't say anything about how dusty the end tables are.

Teach your child how to make strawberry jam.

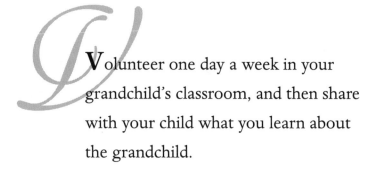

Volunteer one day a week in your grandchild's classroom, and then share with your child what you learn about the grandchild.

Tack down that loose carpeting on his basement stairs.

Have an artist do an oil portrait from your child's best wedding picture.

When you're in your daughter's house, if she silences an upset child with a sugary, commercial confection an hour before dinner, remember that sometimes "Peace at any cost" is a reasonable goal, and refrain from pointing out that Twinkies are not one of the Major Food Groups.

Don't give your grandson that drum set for his birthday.

Go for a long walk together through the old neighborhood. Talk about Mrs. Oldham's crazy cats and the time the tree blew over and smashed the Rasmussens' garage roof.

When your kid gives you a wallet for your birthday, be sure to use it.

Buy them big fluffy bath towels.

Pretend you don't notice when he sneaks chocolate chip cookie dough.

Have Alfred the teddy bear professionally cleaned, and give him a new home at your adult kid's house.

Give her spare keys to her car and house.

Tell your son how pleased you are with the way he turned out. Don't assume he knows. Say it.

If she says she doesn't want to talk about what's upsetting her, drop it. Don't try to pry it out of her. Give her privacy and space.

Give him a teakettle to replace the dented one with the busted whistle.

Buy her a pack of elegant but disposable paper guest towels, so she can quit having to wash and iron the linen ones.

Mount snapshots in an album, but don't leave it at that; next to each picture, tape in a little typed narrative.

Make him gingerbread from scratch.

Give her the key to your beach house.

Pass along Grandma's crystal punchbowl *before* it goes through probate.

Give her your special potato-masher—
the kind they don't sell anymore.

Paint a nice snowscape on a mailbox and give it to
your kids as a housewarming gift.

Slip an "I love you" note into her
purse next time she visits.

Make a family timeline that isn't confined to births, graduations, and other such momentous occasions. Include the time the waitress in the Coulee City cafe asked if you all were okay because you were laughing so hard, and the time Binky played with the dead skunk, and the noteworthy time that Uncle Buck dressed up as a clown and showed up unexpectedly on stilts at your daughter's birthday party.

Let him lick the beaters . . . and the bowl.

Give your kids a videotape of you and your spouse reminiscing about the years before the kids were born—and the first five years after they started coming along.

Go watch your kid play Big Guys League summer softball, even though your official responsibility for doing such things ended thirty years ago with Little League.

The next time she comes over to visit, make her All-Time Favorite dessert from childhood.

Make funny captions for some of his baby pictures, and turn the collection into a comical booklet.

Pass along the paperbacks that you really enjoyed.

Don't get impatient when she details every stroke she took on that 460-yard dogleg sixteenth hole.

Make a collection of the wonderful ways that she said things when she was a little kid. After all, you and your spouse are the only people on Earth who know that she called a screwdriver "kookawoo" or your pen and pencil set "bana banzu."

Give him an envelope full of postage stamps.

153

Tell him that if more people were the kind of father he is, there would be far fewer messed-up kids in the world.

Get a "personal 800" number so your kids can call home at your expense without having to call collect.

During one of her visits, surprise her by polishing and shining her shoes.

FROM *Parents* TO *Kids*

Of course your (little) kids know you love them. You say so to them all the time—don't you? In childhood, that reassurance is needed most of all, and most (alas, not all!) parents remember to give it. It's just natural at tuck-in time to whisper, "I love you," into your sleepy little guy's or girl's ear, and there are plenty of other times when the words probably come naturally to your lips.

But, as we've said throughout the book, it takes more than words; it takes deeds. You say, "I love you," as much by what you *do* as what you *say.* You say it when you sit at his bedside an extra half-hour on a night when he's sure the monsters will get him (provided you know he's not just using a bedtime-stalling tactic). You say it (even if he doesn't realize it) when you tuck him in and read him a long story, even though the dishes haven't been washed yet, you've brought work home from the office, you have three phone calls to return, and you've got a splitting headache on top of that. You even say, "I love you," when you offer him a carrot instead of the fattening snack he's asked for . . . but of course he won't realize till he's older that that was a demonstration of love too.

Fortunately there are plenty of things you can do for her that she'll recognize *now* as ways to say, "I love you." There are many ways to get the message across that he'll hear and understand *now.* And the best part is, these little touches pay a double dividend: Not only are you enriching your kids' childhood now, you're creating memories they'll treasure when they're older. When he thinks back and remembers how Mom always made up her own bedtime stories that no other kid got to hear, or how Dad invented a new game and taught it to him so that he could teach his friends (and feel special and important as a result), he'll have warm memories that glow and light his heart through-out his life. (You'll be setting an example for his way-in-the-future parenting days, as well.)

So go ahead . . . do something special for your child. *Special* things don't have to be *big* things. For instance, little private rituals are spe-cial—a special handshake or modified hug, for instance, that's just between Dad and John, or a silly verbal exchange you repeat every night before bed. These things don't cost money; all they require is time and a little thought. But the dividends they pay—both now and in future warm memories—will be big.

Short on ideas for how to show your child you love him or her? Fortunately, we have some ideas for you. Read on.

*P*ut an "I love you" note in his lunchbox along with the sandwich.

Write a weekly letter on the subject of "What You Did That Made Me Proud This Week," including accomplishments both major and minor. It could be a good grade on a test or report card, a kind deed you noticed, an honest effort (whether or not successful) to try something new, an improvement in table manners, or any other large or small thing your child did that made you proud.

163

Take your child on a picnic,
just the two of you.

Braid pine needles together. Though braiding or weaving pine needles can be part of a result-oriented activity in which you're making something out of the needles, it can also be one of those lazy pastimes that is delightful to do just for fun. You don't have to wind up with a basket, lanyard, or bracelet—you can take great pleasure just weaving pine needles together for the fun of it . . . and for the pleasure of doing something together.

Give him a book of coupons, guaranteed redeemable within 24 hours of presentation. The coupons can be traded for a back rub, 30 minutes of pushing in the swing, a story read aloud, a 15-minute sit-down with cookies and milk, a time watching his favorite cartoon together, and whatever else you can think of.

Write to your child's favorite sports player, singer, or actor and request an autographed picture for him.

Say "I love you" to him by letting him rearrange his room.

Take some time to look for four-leaf clovers together, or to blow on dandelion fluff and scatter it to the wind.

Spray paint an "I love you" message on a stepping stone in the back yard, or plant a flowerbed in such a way that when the flowers come up, they spell out her name.

Let him pop as many balloons as he wants.

Read your kid's favorite story (again!) without complaining or trying to get him to accept an alternate.

167

Call his favorite radio station and dedicate a song request to him.

FROM PARENTS TO KIDS

Spend an afternoon together playing miniature golf.

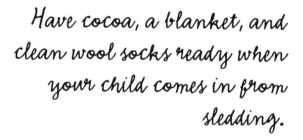

Have cocoa, a blanket, and clean wool socks ready when your child comes in from sledding.

Arrange for your child's best friend to come over to spend the night . . . and keep it a surprise, a secret until the doorbell rings and the friend is there with a big smile and an overnight bag.

Let your child polish her toenails with wild colors.

Give her a fancy-bordered certificate proclaiming her "Best Kid in the World."

Play catch until your child says it's time to stop.

169

Cut "I love you" into the side of an orange that goes in your child's lunch-box.

Put together a "time capsule" for your newborn child, to be opened when he turns eighteen, graduates from school, gets married, or at some other significant milestone of your choosing. Into the capsule—which could be an ordinary box—put such items as

- Copies of her birth announcements (the one you mailed out and the one in the local paper)

- A local paper from the day the child was born

- A few magazines from the time of his birth, showing current fashions, hairstyles, car models, prices

- A list of your wishes and aspirations for the child

- Current photos of yourselves and of any siblings of the newborn

- Photos of your house and the newborn child's room

- A list of people who attended any religious ceremony (baptism, bris, christening, dedication) for the newborn

- The wristband or anklet from the hospital

- A photocopy of the birth certificate

- A photocopy of the hospital bill for delivery

- A packet of sports trading cards, including some of the year's major players

- Anything else relevant to the year or to your child's birth that you can think of.

Spend an unplanned half-hour with your child . . . a half-hour that isn't spent helping him with his homework or overseeing chores or room cleaning, but is devoted entirely to unexpected fun.

Make her bed for her.

Give your child a chestnut. Let him discover the simple pleasure of holding and rubbing a chestnut, the fun of playing old-fashioned games with one. From something as simple as a chestnut, he can learn the truth of the cliché that "the best things in life are free." (Other candidates for teaching the same lesson include a smooth stone, a red and gold maple leaf perfect in its fragility, or an outrageously blue, jagged-edged half of a robin's egg.)

Leave an "I love you" note on her pillow.

 Reserve a little section of the garden for your child to plant and tend.

Let your child build a blanket tent in the living room . . . without bugging him about how he's got to be sure to clean up the mess.

Put up a birdhouse or bird feeder in your yard and watch together as the birds come to it to roost or feed.

Use invisible ink to write a "secret message" to your child—such as "I love you because _____." Lemon juice works fine for this purpose. Write your message with a stylus, a toothpick, or the pointed "wrong" end of a pen, dipping it into the lemon juice to write with. To view the secret message, your child needs only to hold the paper near a light bulb. The heat will make the "invisible ink" reappear.

Give your child a chameleon in an aquarium.

Draw a family tree to help your child understand who all those relatives are and how they're each related to her, and to each other. It will not only help un-confuse your child, it will foster a sense of belonging as well as a sense of family pride.

Tell your child what his best qualities are and what you really love about him.

Ask her advice on a problem you're trying to solve.

Start a scrapbook for your child, including tickets and brochures from things she's done. Show her that you think the things she does are important.

Go fly a kite together.

Take him out in the backyard at night and tell him ghost stories.

On your computer, type in your child's name at the top of a page, using a large, fancy typeface if possible.

Print out ten copies, or make ten photocopies that he can use as stationery for writing to friends (or relatives). Show your child you think he is important enough and old enough to have his own stationery.

Make up a simple story featuring your child as the heroine. Tell it to her as a bedtime story, and make your child feel like a VIP. Type it up and present the child with the printed version.

Make a tree house so your child has a special place to go that she can call her own.

Write your child's name in vertical capital letters like this:

T

O

M

and think of an applicable complimentary attribute beginning with each letter of the child's name. Write it out like this:

> **T**alented at baseball
>
> **O**riginal thinker
>
> **M**akes great model airplanes

Make a mud patch in the corner of the back yard and let your child play in the mud to his heart's content.

Let your child choose the menu for tonight's supper.

Take some souvenir or artifact from an important and treasured part of the child's life (a Scouting badge, a snapshot from the Yellowstone trip, a writing project that earned a smiley-face and two gold stars) and create a distinguished display of it—

framed, shadow-boxed, or otherwise mounted or presented. Allow the child some say in whether it's hung in the hallway or the child's room.

Let him turn the hose on you.

Let him lick the beaters when you're baking.

Send your child a secret message encoded in a simple substitution code (for example, A = B, B = C, C = D). In just one or two encoded sentences, tell why you're proud of your child. Above the sentence, write the "key" so the child will know how to decode the message and will be able to read of your pride in him or her.

When your child is scared at night, leave the hall light on and the door open a crack, and don't say anything critical or negative.

Let your child choose what station the car radio's set to for the next half-hour of the trip.

Attend that stuffed-animal tea party.

Make a treasure hunt, with maps, clues at crucial locations, and really cool treasures that nobody could ever accuse of being practical or sensible.

Let your kid sleep in your bed—special treat, this time only—the next time your spouse is out of town.

*Arrange a special Getaway
Weekend . . . just you and
your kid. No spouse . . .
and (especially) no
little brother!*

Take your child shopping wherever he wants to go
. . . and be patient.

Provide a storage box into which your child's noteworthy drawings, schoolwork, projects, and other creations go. Not only will this repository be a wonderful archive, valued throughout adulthood, but it becomes a focus for sentiment and reminiscence even during childhood. On days when your kid is home sick from school, a look through the box can be the source of feeling better.

Take part in a water balloon fight when asked.

Let your child play with a flashlight, and don't bug her about conserving the batteries.

Let the child choose which route you'll take home from the grocery store.

Let her feed the baby.

Let him name the new dog.

Give your child a bouquet of dandelions, or other wildflowers from your yard, neighborhood vacant lot, or nearby pasture.

Go to the zoo.

Send your kid a postcard every day that you're on that business trip.

Make a cassette tape of yourself reading or telling some of your child's favorite stories.

Pretend there's no electricity, and
spend the evening doing cozy things by
candlelight.

Let your teenage daughter give you a makeover.

Let your child wear whatever silly
sock combination she wants.

Buy him a bunk bed so he can have friends sleep
over.

Show her how to make paper dolls—and stick around to color them with her.

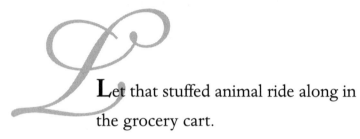

Let that stuffed animal ride along in the grocery cart.

Let him dress himself in the morning, no matter how offbeat the combination, as long as it's weather-appropriate.

Give your kid an official "I'm Completely at Your Disposal" hour every Tuesday afternoon.

Work together to make a little sugar-cube house, barn, or igloo. Use the cubes as bricks. For mortar, mix a thin cake or cookie icing—powdered sugar and butter with milk, juggling the proportions till you have a paste that can be easily spread and will perform the binding of one sugar cube "brick" to another.

If you're going to be away for a night, leave an audiotape of your going-to-bed routine with the child. The tape can include such real-time interactions as "Okay; turn off the tape now, and go brush your teeth; then turn it on when you get back." A "Good night, I love you" message can be at the end of the tape.

Provide a gift for each day of the trip your child is taking. Flashlight the first day. Colorful fanny pack the next day. Giant chocolate bar the next. Book of puzzles the next.

Surprise your kid by showing up at school and spiriting him away for a special lunch date at a restaurant.

Provide the mechanical help that makes it possible for your child to write, illustrate, and bind his or her own book.

Teach your child to play the recorder, pennywhistle, or harmonica.

Relax the quota on the number of tub toys allowed in the bath.

Buy your kid a helmet for bicycling.

Spend special time with each kid, separately and individually. Ask about the child's day. Take a walk. Collect leaves or stones on the walk.

Get your child a library card.

193

*Let her have four friends over
for a pajama party.*

Allow your child access to a videocamera—
whether yours or rented—and help her make her
own movie.

Read to your child.

Proudly display your kid's bouquet, even though
it's mostly dandelions.

Have a picnic with a red and white checked table-cloth . . . in the middle of the living room floor.

Pop popcorn and watch your child's favorite movie together.

Display the child's artwork not just on the refrigerator, but in a special place on the mantel, too.

195

Make a family tree that has a picture with each name.

Dust off those bikes and go for a ride together.

Get together and drop pebbles off a bridge into the creek.

Check under the bed for monsters one more time, and show no exasperation.

Look through their school yearbooks with them, and let them talk about all the things that are interesting and important to them.

Have your kid tell a story into the tape recorder. Transcribe the words onto paper, illustrate the adventures, make a colorful cover of construction paper, and present the little one with his or her first published work.

Visit a couple of rummage sales till you can fill an old suitcase with hats, clothes, and other dress-up or fantasy clothing possibilities—perhaps even wings and a crown—to give to your little princess.

Plant a tree when Baby is born, and take his or her picture in front of the tree every year. Show them both growing. And if you move away . . . well, that tree gives a good reason to come back to visit the old neighborhood as often as possible!

Start a diary when each child is born. Write something about the child every day of his or her life. Read excerpts from the book every year on the child's birthday, or at Christmas (or any other meaningful occasion). When the child grows up and moves out, give the diary to him or her.

Take all those agates and pretty rocks that she picked up when you were walking on the beach to a rock shop. Have them tumble-polished. If you're really looking for a loud statement of "I love you,"

you can have the polished stones set into a very, very special bracelet or necklace.

Don't tell your son he's too old to cry.

Make doll clothes that match your little girl's clothes. Being able to dress her doll the same way she is dressed will be a great delight.

FROM *Kids* TO *Parents*

Whether you're nine or sixteen or some other age, you know how warm and good you feel when Mom or Dad tells you, "I love you," and you feel good, too, when they *do* something nice or special for you. Though you may not think about it in so many words, you know that the nice things that Mom and Dad do for you are things they do because they love you.

When Mom or Dad says to you, "I love you," you probably answer back, "I love you." Moms and dads like to hear "I love you" from their kids just as much as kids like to hear it from their parents.

And, just the way you like it when they *do* something that says "I love you," your parents like it, too, when *you* do something loving for them, something that shows them how much you think of them and love them.

It's easier for a parent to show a child that he loves the child than the other way around. After all, your parents can do more for you than you can do for them. And they have more money to buy you little presents; your piggy bank or bank account may not have a lot of money in it.

Fortunately, there are still some ways you can show Mom and Dad that you love them. Some of them are more suitable for younger kids, while others are better for teenagers. Remember, you don't have to buy expensive presents or even make something difficult or elaborate with your own hands. You can make a

simple little present that shows you were thinking of your parents—one or the other or both of
them. You can do something nice for them that
shows your love.

Just making a piece of toast for Mom or
cleaning up your room *before* she has to ask you
will show her you love her and want to make
her happy. Writing a story about why your dad is
the greatest, or offering to help him pull weeds in
the garden will show him, too, that you love him
and want to help him and make him feel good.

And these things *will* make your parents feel
good. These things and others. We have some
suggestions; just keep reading. You may even
think of things yourself that you can do or make
for Mom or Dad. Remember, the important

thing is to let them know you love them, and to do it not just by *telling* them but also by *showing* them. They'll get the message.

So go ahead . . . read the suggestions that follow this, and then do something loving for Mom and Dad today (and on lots of other days, too)!

*W*rite "I love you" in large letters on a big piece of construction paper, and draw some pictures on the page too. Now cut the construction paper up into pieces like those of a jig-saw puzzle. Give your mom or dad the puzzle. They'll like what they find when they put it together!

Ask your parents to tell you stories of their child-hood.

If you're old enough to handle wire carefully, make a button bouquet, using florist wire for stems. Each flower can be made of one button, or two or three buttons. Put the biggest buttons on the bottom so the colors of all the buttons show. Include an "I love you" note. (These flowers can stand up in a small glass or vase, or their stems can be stuck into clay or Styrofoam.)

Cut a piece of paper—dark-colored construction paper works best, but any will do—so it is exactly the size of the lens of your folks' flashlight. Cut a heart out of the center of the paper. Carefully tape the paper over the flashlight lens. The result will be a heart-shaped beam of light that says "I love you" in an unusual way.

Perhaps your parents have given you the fun of a Treasure Hunt; well, it's time to return the favor! Write clues, or directions, that will lead your mom and dad to different places in the house . . . and at each place, there will be a new clue, telling them a new place to go. At the end of the Treasure Hunt is the Treasure . . . a note from you telling them how much you love them.

You can make your clues easy ("Look under the cushion on the couch") or very family-specific ("The next clue will be found in the same place that Mom found her checkbook when Timmy was a toddler and he hid it"). You can make them playful ("The witch who wants to hurt Hansel and Gretel would find the next clue pretty quickly" points to the oven) or poetic ("To find the next clue to the treasure/ Look in the cup you use to measure").

Say "I love you" by staying quiet when Dad's taking a nap, even though you've got a lot of really cool toys that make noise.

Ask for permission, then match up and line up all your mom's shoes in the closet. Likewise your dad's socks in his dresser drawer.

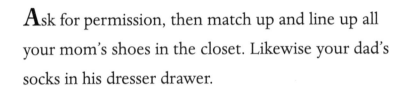

French braid Mom's hair, and give her a manicure.

Make a ceramic mug, vase, or plaque on which a special, personalized "I love you" message is engraved, painted, or glazed. This isn't like getting a "World's Best Parents" mug at the gift store—the words on this one are words that only you could say, and that you put there yourself, especially for your mom or dad.

213

Get that drink of water in the middle of the night yourself, without waking anybody up.

If there are several of you in the family, how about saying "I love you" to your parents by giving them a day with absolutely no fighting among you all . . . guaranteed!

Don't ask your mom whether Kim can stay overnight if Kim is standing there.

Thank your parents again for something nice that they did for you a while back. Show them you haven't forgotten.

Take a bath without being told.

Draw a certificate saying "World's Greatest Mom" (or " . . . Dad"). Color in yellow (or gold) an official-looking seal, and draw two red ribbons hanging down from it. Sign it with your name at the bottom.

215

Make Mom a tissue carnation. Cut three pieces of tissues (such as Kleenex) so that they're square instead of rectangular. If they're two-ply tissue, separate the tissue into its two pieces. Now put the tissue layers one on top of the other. Using a pencil or pen, make an indentation (not a hole) in the center, and bring all the edges up so that they're squeezed together. Remove the pen. Hold the "flower" at the bottom and separate the squeezed-together edges into the shape of a carnation. (If you can use pink tissue, it will be even prettier and more realistic.)

Do the laundry even though it's not your turn to do it.

Show your parents you love them by making a "Home Sweet Home" sign. You can use crayons, paints, felt-tips, colored pencils, or whatever; you can embroider the message; or you can find some other way to express your appreciation for the home you have and the people you love who make it such a special place.

Clean your room without being asked.

217

Make an "I love you" card for your parents. Homemade cards are always a treasure and always say, "I love you." They're much more special and much more personal than cards from the store. On the front of your card you can put a drawing of your family, including your pets. Inside, besides "I love you," you can also write something special that your family says often. Or you can write, "I love you because_____" and give one or more reasons that you love your mom, your dad, or both.

Do the dishes when it's not your turn.

Watch that corny old movie that your mom or dad has been trying for so long to get you to watch. (And be prepared for a nice surprise—you're likely to find that they knew what they were talking about when they said you would love this film . . . even though it's in black and white!)

Make little "I love you" notes and leave them in places where your mom and dad will find them, but not right away—in the garden shed, under the bathroom sink, in a shoe not often worn, in a file drawer. It'll be nice to have these "love surprises" catching them when they least expect it. (Don't put them in any drawer or anyplace else where you're not supposed to go!)

Get your hair cut.

Ask whether your folks kept any of the baby clothes you had when you were really little. When you're looking at these relics of the past, ask them to tell you about what it was like where you lived when you were born, what kinds of memories they have of those days, and so on. It'll be interesting . . .

and it's a nice way of reminding them that you love them as much as they love you.

Pool your allowance with your sister's or brother's allowance, and treat your folks to a meal at a nice restaurant . . . while you kids stay home and let them enjoy a little time off by themselves.

221

Ask if you can help by straightening out or organizing a drawer.

For a birthday, Christmas or Chanukah, or Mother's or Father's Day present, or a present for any other occasion, or for no occasion at all, give your mom or dad some homemade coupons. These coupons aren't good for 10¢ off on bread at the supermarket. These coupons are good for chores. They'll say things like "Good for Raking the Yard" or "Good for Doing the Dishes." When your parents want, they can turn in a coupon to you, and you'll then have to make good on the coupon and do the chore in question.

Get letter-beads at the craft store and make your mom a bracelet. Spell out "I Love You" or "World's Best Mom" with the beads.

Come home even before you're supposed to.

Wrap your next gift to your parents (or grand-parents) in gift wrap you've made by making finger-paint impressions of your hands on plain brown wrapping paper. Use lots of colors.

Take the dog for a walk without being asked.

Record a birthday greeting to your mom or dad on a tape recorder. Say "Happy Birthday" or sing "Happy Birthday to You," and say what year it is that you're recording this message. Add anything else to it that you want. Every year, at the end of last year's tape, record a new birthday greeting. Your parents will treasure this tape.

Run up and give your mom a big hug and tell her you love her—not at some special moment, but just when you figure she could use something very happy and special in her day.

Take your disk out of the computer when you're through.

Turn off the TV, or the video game, and ask your parents if they'll go for a walk with you. It'll be fun, and a great way to share the love that makes you a family.

Write your mom a poem.

Have a parade with all your brothers and sisters. Make banners that tell your parents how great they are. (It's probably best to have this parade outdoors, so you don't have to worry about the banners knocking lamps off the end tables.) Your banners might say "You're the Best, Mom and Dad" or "Number One Parents."

Plant and take care of a small flower garden or flower box that will make your home a more pleasant place to be.

Write and illustrate one of the stories that your mom or dad tells about when they were kids. (And let them know that you love hearing about the days when they were your age!)

Clean out the kitty litter box without being asked.

Paint a sign, using one of Mom's or Dad's favorite pieces of advice as the sentiment. It can be a one-word reminder, such as "Patience," if that's what

Mom seems to say the most, or "Think Before You Speak," or whatever Mom or Dad seem to say most often.

Don't bring wiggly things into the house.

If you're old enough, wash the family car. (Get permission first and be sure you're using the right stuff for the job. Ruining the paint on the car isn't the best way to say, "I love you," even if your intentions are great!)

Share your excitement about books by reading to your parents from the books or stories that you especially like. (Maybe you can turn them into huge Harry Potter or Encyclopedia Brown fans!)

Clean out your pockets before putting your clothes into the laundry basket.

Draw a really colorful picture of a butterfly or a sun or something that looks bright and happy. Give it to your mom or dad (to put on the refrigerator) and say, "This is because you make my day bright and happy."

Remember how you promised to keep the cage clean if your folks would let you get that hamster, parakeet, or gerbil? Clean that cage!

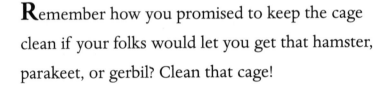

Wear your helmet when you ride your bike.

Tell the cook in your family that it was a great dinner, even if it wasn't your favorite. And offer to help with the dishes.

When the answer is "no,"
don't beg or whine.

Make an Olympics-style medal (a medallion on a ribbon) to celebrate what a special person your mom or dad is. The medal can be made from something simple like a pill-bottle lid, with the words written with a marker. It can be made of clay or ceramic, with the letters written on it with a special tool. For that matter, it isn't even necessary that the medal have words on it—the idea of thanking your parents and honoring and praising them is what really counts.

Wipe your feet.

Acknowledgments

The authors gratefully appreciate the help of:
Cathy Bobb, Lenna Buissink, and Tiffany Buissink.

About the Authors

Cynthia MacGregor, the author of nearly forty published books, is a full-time freelance writer and editor. Her professional work includes stints as a publisher and theater editor/reviewer. Cynthia considers herself one of the luckiest people in the world and says, "There is no one in the world I'd want to trade lives with." She lives in Lantana, Florida. Her Web site is *www.CynthiaMacGregor.com.*

Vic Bobb, a native of Pullman, Washington, is Professor of English at Whitworth College, Spokane. A freelance writer for more than twenty years, he has published articles on topics as various as *The Beverly Hillbillies,* archaeology, rodeo, and Robert Frost.

To Our Readers

Conari Press publishes books on topics ranging from spirituality, personal growth, and relationships to women's issues, parenting, and social issues. Our mission is to publish quality books that will make a difference in people's lives—how we feel about ourselves and how we relate to one another. We value integrity, compassion, and receptivity, both in the books we publish and in the way we do business.

As a member of the community, we donate our damaged books to nonprofit organizations, dedicate a portion of our proceeds from certain books to charitable causes, and continually look for new ways to use natural resources as wisely as possible.

Our readers are our most important resource, and we value your input, suggestions, and ideas about what you would like to see published. Please feel free to contact us, to request our latest book catalog, or to be added to our mailing list.

2550 Ninth Street, Suite 101
Berkeley, California 94710-2551
800-685-9595 • 510-649-7175
fax: 510-649-7190
e-mail: conari@conari.com
http://www.conari.com

239